Why doesn't Alice talk at school?

A storybook to read to friends and the class about Selective Mutism

Lucy Nathanson

ISBN 978-1-78972-652-7

Illustrations by Hricha Toplewar

Acknowledgements

I am beyond grateful to have the opportunity to write another book to help children with selective mutism.

I would like to thank my mum for sitting with me in a traditional Polish cottage, brainstorming ideas for the new character's name, and for choosing 'Alice'.

Thank you to my sister for always being there for me, and for being supportive of my ideas.

My amazing friends, and my tribe of magic makers, who are always happy to listen to my projects, and encourage me to reach even higher.

For Hricha, my wonderful illustrator, who shared my excitement and vision when Alice was just an idea.

For parents of children with selective mutism, who are often my biggest cheerleaders, supporting me in my mission to reach as many children with selective mutism as I can, worldwide.

For children with selective mutism, whom this is all for.
You are my biggest teachers; seeing you overcome your fears gives me the inspiration and strength to be brave and overcome my own.

Thank you.

Contents

Information for Adults

This is a storybook that can be read to the class and to friends to help children to understand what selective mutism is and how to support a child that they know with selective mutism.

Selective mutism is an anxiety disorder whereby a child is unable to talk in some situations or to specific people. Commonly, children with selective mutism are unable to talk at school.

In order to support a child with selective mutism in beginning to use their voice, the first step is to create a supportive environment. In various ways, peers, often unintentionally, maintain the selective mutism, and make it harder for the child to begin to use their voice.

The aim of this book is to help explain to peers what the child is experiencing and to provide them with the essential do's and don'ts in a child-friendly way.

Often, the child with selective mutism has been the 'person who doesn't talk' for such a long time that peers are used to this. It becomes part of the child's identity and this label can limit progress.

Peers, out of curiosity, sometimes make comments, such as "why don't you talk?" or "when are you going to talk?" These are innocent questions; however, the child with selective mutism doesn't know the answer to these questions. They are experiencing anxiety and such focus on their inability to talk makes it harder for them to begin to use their voice.

Children with selective mutism are often fearful of how peers would respond if they were to speak. Naturally, it is a very exciting moment for peers when the child with selective mutism speaks for the first time. Their automatic response may be to clap, cheer or say, "YOU SPOKE!", "SHE CAN TALK!", "HE SPOKE!", "WOW!"

A child with selective mutism is experiencing high anxiety and thus, such comments would likely halt their ability to continue. It is therefore important for peers to be briefed to act completely normally should the child speak.

Adults can use this book as a tool to explain these important messages to the class and to friends. This book should be read without the child with selective mutism present. This will allow peers to have their questions answered in a safe space, help them to gain some understanding of what the child is experiencing and for them to know what to do and not to do to help their friend.

Lucy Nathanson, the author of this book, also has videos on the Confident Children YouTube channel that can be shown to the class as another way to begin a conversation with peers. There is a video for younger children and a video for older children.

The video for younger children is called: *Selective Mutism: video for children (to show to the class) by Lucy Nathanson.* The video for older children is called: *Selective Mutism - video for older children and teenagers (to show to the class) by Lucy Nathanson.*

It is only appropriate to read this book to children if they have an awareness of the child not talking or they have made comments in the past, and there is the possibility that they would make a fuss should the child speak for the first time. If these factors do not apply, it may not be necessary to read this book to them.

The goal is that peers finish this book with a sense of understanding about their friend. They know not to ask specific questions and they know what to do should their friend use their voice one day. This approach will help to create a supportive class environment for the child with selective mutism.

Why doesn't Alice talk at school?

A storybook to read to friends and the class about Selective Mutism

LUCY NATHANSON

www.confidentchildren.co.uk

Mr Follows walked into his classroom after lunch and sat down in his teacher's chair. It had been a busy day with lots of learning; the class had already had story time, a music lesson, learnt new spellings, and they'd also done a lot of running around today!

It was now time for Mr Follows to talk to the class about Alice.

Alice wasn't at school today. Alice was a lovely girl. Her best friend was Lauren. Alice loved colouring in pictures using all the colours of the rainbow!

Once the children came back into the classroom after playtime, they all sat on the carpet.

Mr Follows looked at the class and said, "Today I want to talk to you about Alice."

James' hand shot up in the air like a rocket.

"Why doesn't Alice talk at school?"

Mr Follows smiled and said,
"Before I answer that question, I would like
to ask you all, what do you find scary?"

Maria said she was scared of spiders.

Oliver said he was scared of heights.

Lauren said she was scared of the dark.

Jacob said he was scared of swimming.

Isabel said she was scared of loud noises.

Joey said he was scared of cats.

Mr Follows looked at the class and said,

"Everyone is scared of something,
and Alice is scared of talking at school.
Do you know how we can help her?"

The children didn't know.

Mr Follows paused for a moment.

"Who thinks we should keep asking Alice why she doesn't talk or when she will talk?"

A few of the children put their hands up.

Mr Follows smiled and said calmly...

Mr Follows paused and smiled again.

"The way that we can help Alice to feel happier at school is to just play with her and not ask her anything about talking. There are lots of ways to have fun with Alice without her needing to talk – does anyone have an idea of things you could do?"

Milly put her hand up. "We could draw a picture together."

Joey said, "We could play catch in the playground if Alice wants to."

Isabel said, "We could talk to her about things without asking her questions."

Mr Follows smiled at the class and said,

"Those are all wonderful ideas. There are lots of ways to have fun with Alice, without her needing to talk."

"So...we all understand that we shouldn't ask Alice why she doesn't talk and we shouldn't ask her when she will talk; instead we should just have fun with Alice and this will help her to feel happier at school."

"That's a great question, Maria!" Mr Follows said. "If Alice talks to you, just act normally and reply to what she said!"
"But what if we are really excited that she spoke?" Maria asked.

Mr Follows smiled again and said, "I'm sure it will be very exciting when Alice speaks, but we shouldn't make a fuss. I want you all to put your best acting hats on and act as if she always spoke. Don't say 'wow!' or 'you talked!'; instead just act normally!"

Mr Follows looked at the class for a moment. "Who is a good actor in this class?" Every child put their hand up. "Great!" said Mr Follows, "when Alice talks to you, I'm going to see who the best actor is and who acts completely normally!"

Milly put her hand up.
"Yes, Milly?" Mr Follows asked.

"Mr Follows, will Alice talk at school one day?"

Mr Follows smiled at all the children.

"Yes, Alice might talk at school one day, but when she is ready."

Questions to ask the class

1. Why do you think your friend doesn't talk at school?

2. Should you ask your friend why they don't talk?

3. Should you ask your friend when they will talk?

4. If your friend talks one day should you say "you talked!" or "wow"?

5. What should you do if your friend talks?

6. Who is a good actor in this class?

The End

Other books by Lucy Nathanson

Understanding Selective Mutism: A Beginner's Guide

This 30-page book is a clear and concise introduction to selective mutism; it is an excellent tool for parents to lend to family members and school staff to help them to gain an understanding of selective mutism in a short amount of time. There are often misconceptions surrounding this condition; the aim of this book is to provide the reader with an understanding of what children with selective mutism are experiencing. This book covers an overview of selective mutism: what selective mutism is and is not, the diagnostic criteria, what causes selective mutism, how to interact with a child with selective mutism and an overview of the treatment methods.

My name is Eliza and I don't talk at school

This beautifully illustrated and positive book is an excellent aid and therapeutic tool for both therapists and parents of primary-age children with selective mutism. Selectively mute children who are aged 6 years and over can also read this book themselves or with an adult. The book opens with a section for adults to read before presenting the story to the child, explaining how best to use the book and the therapeutic approach to helping children with selective mutism, as well as including useful discussion questions.

Eliza's charming story then follows. In the first half, Eliza describes how she feels in different situations, both at home and at school - feelings that will resonate with many children with selective mutism. In the second half, we discover how she begins to overcome her fear with small steps and easy methods that parents and therapists can adopt. With delightful artwork, this story will help children with selective mutism feel as though they are not alone, as well as offering parents and professionals a way to begin a conversation with the child about their selective mutism and suggest the steps to help them.

For more content on selective mutism and to find out about the support we offer, see:

www.confidentchildren.co.uk

and the Facebook page:

Confident Children – Selective Mutism Therapy

To be the first to know about any new content, subscribe to our website and YouTube channel.

Printed in Poland
by Amazon Fulfillment
Poland Sp. z o.o., Wrocław

51091685R10028